STORYBOOKS FOR *Caring* PARENTS

Tired, But Not Too Tired (to finish)

Dave Jackson

Illustrated by Susan Lexa

Chariot Books
DAVID C. COOK PUBLISHING CO.

To Carrie

Chariot Books is an imprint of David C. Cook Publishing Co.
David C. Cook Publishing Co., Elgin, Illinois 60120
David C. Cook Publishing Co., Weston, Ontario

TIRED, BUT NOT TOO TIRED
© 1985 by Dave Jackson for the text and Susan Lexa for the illustrations.
All rights reserved. Except for brief excerpts for review purposes, no part of this book may be reproduced or used in any form without written permission from the publisher.
Cover photo by Bakstad Photographics

First printing, 1985
Printed in the United States of America
89 88 87 86 85   5 4 3 2 1

Library of Congress Cataloging in Publication Data

Jackson, Dave.
  Tired, but not too tired (to finish).

  (Storybooks for caring parents)
  Summary: Stories with accompanying Scripture quotations and discussion questions demonstrate the effectiveness of persevering and finishing such projects as cleaning a room, making a gift for a relative, and bailing out a leaky boat.
  1. Perseverance (Ethics)—Juvenile literature. 2. Christian life—1960—Juvenile literature.
[1. Perseverance (Ethics) 2. Christian life] I. Lexa, Susan, ill. II. Title. III. Series.
BJ1553.P4J33   1985   241'.4   84-27454
ISBN 0-89191-963-5

Scripture references identified (NIV) are from the New International Version; those identified (TEV) are from Today's English Version.

Contents

For Parents

Story 1
The Deal 7

Story 2
A Little at a Time 15

Story 3
Leaky Boat 23

For Parents

It is astounding how many times an infant will try to roll over and fail but keep on trying. What happens to that perseverance by the time the child is five or six? Too often a child will expend just a little effort and then claim to be too tired to finish.

This Storybook for Caring Parents is written to help you develop perseverance in your children. The introductory section offers insights and suggestions for you, the parent. The three stories that follow are for you to read aloud to your children. Let "tired, but not too tired to finish" become a slogan they will remember and use.

The Deal

Carrie and her friend Faye want to spend the night together. Their mothers say okay . . . if both girls will clean their rooms before supper. The girls agree to the deal in an instant and with great excitement. But before the job is done, they both get tired, take a break to watch TV, and almost miss their deadline.

When Carrie's mother notices that the girls are having trouble finishing, she suggests that they work together, first doing one girl's room and then the other's. Cooperation is the key that gives the girls enough support to finish the job in time.

Sharing hard tasks is one way to get through them. Somehow the job seems easier when we work together, and it's good for children to learn this. The Scripture at the end of this story (II Corinthians 8:11) speaks of finishing a task. The context is Paul's writing to encourage the Corinthian believers to finish the job of helping the believers in Jerusalem—a prime example of the kind of cooperation and sharing taught by the story.

There's another useful principle in the story. Sometimes called "Grandmother's Rule," it's an incentive approach that helps kids do tasks they'd rather ignore. Instead of making a threat ("You can't have a sleepover because your room is dirty"), try the more effective positive approach (*"If you finish the room before supper, then you can have the sleepover"*). You'll be pleased with how well it works.

We all work hardest for the things that we really want. Maybe that's one reason an infant will work for days just to master rolling over. When your child is really motivated, and the task is manageable if he or she can just get over the hump, that is when your encouragement to keep on can be the most helpful.

A Little at a Time

Carrie decides to make Grandpa a very special Christmas present—a calendar with a drawing for each month. She enjoys the project for the first six pictures, but then she is tired and can't think of anything to draw for the rest. Mother suggests that hard tasks are easier when one does a little bit at a time. Carrie tries doing one picture each night, and in a week the project is done and ready for Christmas.

Frustration comes easily for children when they take on a project that is too big for the time they imagine it will take. This is true of making a set of calendar pictures or learning to ice-skate. Children (and adults) often underestimate what is required to complete a task. If a child does not learn to readjust expectations or break a job down into manageable parts, he or she may grow into an adult who can't follow through.

It's important that the expectations parents have for their children be appropriately achievable. The mother in this story avoids the error of forcing Carrie to finish the whole project the same day it was started. Neither does she allow Carrie to give up, and she doesn't rush in to do it for her. Accomplishments in the face of small doses of frustration help a child develop perseverance. Failures or too much frustration reinforce defeatism and despair.

Enhance children's perseverance by helping them make wise choices about the things they try and the subgoals needed to complete the task. Protect them from being totally overwhelmed, but don't be afraid of encouraging a little stretching. And allow them to make some mistakes. Maintaining this balance is difficult, but it can be done.

Leaky Boat

On a fishing trip in an old, leaky boat, Carrie and her dad get caught in bad weather. Dad has to row them back against the wind, and the going gets very rough. Water seeps into the boat, adding weight and making the rowing harder. Carrie's job is to bail out the water from the bottom of the boat, but fear and fatigue make her nearly too tired to finish.

They pray for God's help, and then Dad suggests that games sometimes help people do hard jobs. They begin to sing while they work, giving Carrie new courage and rhythm to keep on bailing till they get safely back to camp.

Besides demonstrating the technique of making a helpful game out of a task, this story shows that parents get tired, too. Dad is just as tired as Carrie, but both must find a way to keep going.

Strengthen your child's perseverance by acknowledging that you, too, sometimes have trouble finishing a tough task. Too often children think parents are omnipotent. When frustration and tiredness strike them, they feel alone in their struggle. Being tired, but not too tired to finish, must be taught by example, too.

Story 1

The Deal

It was a sunny afternoon, and Carrie and Faye were hot from jumping rope. They sat down on the front steps of their apartment building to talk.

"Let's ask if we can have a sleepover with just the two of us tonight," Faye said.

The girls ran inside and up the stairs to their apartments, which were just across the hall from each other.

"Mom," called Carrie, bursting through the door, "can Faye and I spend the night together?"

"Let's see what Faye's mom thinks," Mom said, walking toward the open front door.

The girls and their mothers met in the hallway. "Well, Faye is supposed to clean her room today. Right now, those girls would get lost in the mess!" teased Faye's mom.

"Oh, Mom, it isn't that bad," said Faye. "I'll get it done this afternoon."

"Now that you mention it," Carrie's mom said, "Carrie's room needs cleaning, too."

"Oh, I'll do it," Carrie said quickly. "Just say yes, okay?"

"Okay," said Mom. Then she turned to Faye's mom. "Why don't the girls have supper at our house and go over to your place to sleep?"

Carrie and Faye jumped up and down and danced around in a circle.

"Now, girls, we're not going to nag you about

your jobs this afternoon. Understood?"

"Don't worry, Mom," said Carrie. "It's a deal."

"You won't have to say a word," promised Faye.

But when Carrie got to her room, she was surprised to see what a mess it was in. She picked up some books and put them on the bookshelf. Then she put all the furniture back into her dollhouse. She picked up a dirty sock and dropped it in the hamper. But there was still tons to do. She stopped and went over to Faye's.

Faye was sitting in the middle of the floor with piles of stuff all around. "I'm tired," she said.

"Me, too," said Carrie. "I didn't think it would take this long."

"Maybe we ought to take a little break and watch TV."

They watched two cartoons. Then Carrie said, "We'd better see how long it is till supper."

Carrie's mom said they had a little more than an hour. Both girls went back to work, but their progress was slow.

Finally Carrie went to the kitchen. "Mom, I've been working for a long time, and it's not done yet. Can't you let us have the sleepover anyway? The room is better."

"No, Carrie. You can have your sleepover only if your rooms are cleaned before supper."

"But, Mom, I'm too tired to do any more."

"Well, sometimes hard jobs are easier when

people work together. You have forty minutes till dinner. Why don't you go help Faye with her room, and then both of you can finish yours."

Carrie went off to tell Faye the plan. Working together, they soon finished Faye's room. Then they ran back to Carrie's apartment.

"How much time, Mom?" called Carrie as they hurried toward her room.

"Fifteen minutes."

"Oh, no. We'll never make it."

"Would you like me to set the kitchen timer?" Mom offered. "You could take it in there and watch it while you work."

The timer ticked away, but the girls nearly flew as they put things away. At last all that was left was making the bed.

Ding! The timer rang, and just then Carrie's mom peeked in. "You've got a few extra minutes," she said. "Daddy just phoned to say he'll be a little late. And I have to change the baby before we eat." She turned to leave, and then poked her head back in. "Hey. The room's looking pretty good."

Soon the bed was made. The girls shook hands and flopped down on the floor. They never knew they could do so much work so fast.

And what a good time they had that night! ∎

From God's Word

Now finish the work, so that your eager willingness to do it may be matched by your completion of it.
—*from II Corinthians 8:11 (NIV)*

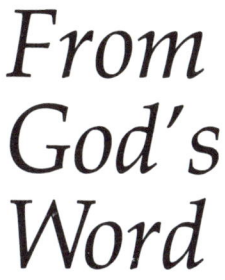

TIRED, BUT NOT TOO TIRED

Think It Through

Ask your children these questions and discuss the answers.

1. How did stopping to watch TV affect finishing the job? Do you think the girls should have taken a break? Why?

2. What did Carrie's mom suggest that helped the girls finish their hard job? Why did it help?

3. After trying so hard, how would the girls have felt if they hadn't finished in time?

4. Can you think of a household chore you have to do that would be easier if you shared it with someone? What job could you help that other person do in exchange?

Story 2

A Little At a Time

Carrie ran home from school and burst in the door. "Mom, can I use your markers?" she called.

"Sure. What are you going to do?"

15

"I want to make Grandpa a picture calendar for Christmas. My teacher gave us all these calendar pages, see? I make a picture for the top and tape the date pages to the bottom."

Carrie got set up with markers and paper at the kitchen table. Then she turned to Mom. "What shall I do for January?" she asked.

"Let's see. January is a winter month, so maybe you could make a picture about winter. But these need to be your ideas, not mine."

Carrie thought for a while. Then she put one of her hands flat on the paper with her fingers together and her thumb sticking out, and traced around it.

A Little at a Time

She traced around her other hand and colored in the two areas with green.

"There," she said proudly. "A pair of mittens for January."

After that Carrie made a valentine for February and flowers for March.

"I've got three done," she announced. "This is easy." *But what should I draw for April?* she wondered. She couldn't think of anything for April, May, or June. July was easy—fireworks to celebrate the birth of her country.

Four pictures were done, but Carrie had been drawing for what seemed like days. She flipped

17

through the other months. *I could make a turkey for Thanksgiving,* she thought, *and a manger for Jesus at Christmas. But what else?*

"I can't think of any more," she said. "I did four and I have ideas for two more, but then I'm stuck."

"Well, do what you can," said Mom.

"But I'm tired," Carrie complained. "And if I can't think of any more, all this work will be for nothing."

"But with two more done, you'll be half finished. That's pretty good, isn't it?" Mom asked.

"I thought I'd be *all* done by now. Half done means there's still a whole lot more to do."

Carrie sat silently looking at her paper for a while. Finally she went to work on the turkey and then the manger scene.

"That's beautiful," said Mom as she walked by.

"But I'm tired, and I haven't thought of anything else," said Carrie angrily. She grabbed a black marker and made a great big X across her

December picture. The beautiful manger scene was ruined. "I'm not going to give Grandpa a Christmas present," she said, bursting into tears.

Mom took Carrie in her arms. "I can see that you're very disappointed," she said. She let Carrie cry for a few minutes and then continued. "You know what? I think you tried to do too big a job for one afternoon. The only way to finish some things is to do a little at a time over a longer period."

"But it's so much work," Carrie moaned.

"Yes," said Mom, "it is a lot of work. But look at how much you did today. If you could do six pictures in one day, surely you could do one a day to finish them. Just take one step at a time."

"Well, I guess I can redo the Christmas one tomorrow. But then what? I still don't have ideas for the rest."

"Don't think about that right now," suggested Mom. "Remember what Jesus said: 'Don't worry about tomorrow, for tomorrow will worry about itself. Each day has enough trouble of its own.' "

After school the next day, Carrie sat down with the markers and did her December page over again. Her new picture of Jesus in the manger was even better than the one she'd done the day before. And while she was doing it, she thought of something she could do for August.

"I was tired, but I guess I'm not too tired to finish, Mom," she said. "Tomorrow I'm going to draw Grandpa and me eating ice-cream cones."

When the week was up, Carrie had finished her calendar by doing just a little at a time. ■

A Little at a Time

From God's Word

Let us not become weary
in doing good,
for at the proper time
we will reap a harvest
if we do not give up.
—from Galatians 6:9 (NIV)

Think It Through

Ask your children these questions and discuss the answers.

1. Why did Carrie get tired of making the pictures for her grandpa?

2. What sometimes happens when people try to do too big a job at one time?
   They can get discouraged and want to quit altogether.

3. Why do you think Carrie's second manger picture was even better than her first?
   When she did the first one, she was all tired out from doing five others. The next day she was fresh and ready to work again.

4. What did Carrie learn about how to do big jobs without getting too tired to finish?

5. Think of two big jobs or hard skills to learn that must be done a little at a time.

Story 3

Leaky Boat

Carrie and her dad pushed their little boat away from the dock. The sun had just come up, and there was a golden fog hanging low over the still lake.

Dad pulled steadily on the oars. They went *creeek*, and *creeek*, and *creeek*, as the old boat glided slowly out of the cove into the larger lake.

Just as they went around the point, Carrie whispered, "Daddy, look." Through a break in the mist she could see a big raccoon busily washing his breakfast in the lake.

"Probably a fish—maybe a bluegill," Dad whispered back.

Carrie watched the ripples move out through the

smooth water like a *V* behind their boat. Suddenly she realized that her foot was wet and cold. There in the bottom of the boat was an inch of water.

"Dad, the boat's leaking. Are we going to sink?"

"It sure enough is leaking," said Dad. "When I pull on the oars, it makes that seam open and a little stream of water comes in. But, no, we won't sink. Grab that bailer and get some of the water out."

Carrie picked up the plastic bucket. Scoop and dump. Scoop and dump. Soon there was only a little water left in the boat.

"We've reached our fishing spot," Dad said.

Carrie had been so busy that she hadn't noticed that they were at the other end of the lake. A slight breeze turned the surface of the water into a shimmering field of diamonds.

Dad helped Carrie put a worm on her hook and toss it near an old bush sticking out of the water. Then he started getting his line ready. Suddenly Carrie felt a tug on her line.

"I think I've got something," she said.

"Wait until it tugs again," said Dad. "Then give your pole a good yank and wind the line in."

Carrie waited, tense with excitement. Her loose line straightened out, and there was another tug. She yanked back on her pole and started to crank the line in, but the fish took off around the back of the boat, pulling her pole with it.

"It's too big for me, Daddy," she cried.

"You can do it. Here, I'll help you." They fought the fish until it was right beside the boat, and then Dad reached down with his net and scooped it up. It was a beautiful bluegill, as big as Dad's hand.

The fishing was good the rest of the morning.

Finally Dad said, "I think we'd better head for home, Carrie. I don't like the look of those clouds, and we've got a long way to row."

He pulled up the anchor, and Carrie lifted their heavy basket of fish into the boat.

"I want you to use that bailer to keep the water out of the boat," Dad said. "Water is heavy, and I don't want to haul any more weight than necessary."

Carrie bailed and Dad rowed, but they didn't seem to be getting very far. Waves slapped the front of the boat, and the wind blew at them.

Carrie was worried. "Are we going to get there, Dad?"

"We'll make it," he said, pulling steadily on.

TIRED, BUT NOT TOO TIRED

"You just keep bailing."

Carrie bailed. Scoop the water, pour it out. Scoop the water, pour it out.

"I'm getting tired, Daddy," she said, as the boat bobbed over the waves.

"Me, too. But we've got a long way to go. We're tired, but not too tired to finish. Right?"

A big wave slapped the front of the boat, and the wind blew spray in Carrie's face. Water seemed to be leaking in faster.

"Dad, are we going to sink? I'm scared."

"No, I think we're okay. But let's pray and ask God to help us. I'd like to get home before your mom starts to worry."

They both prayed as they continued to row and bail. When they had finished, Dad said, "Carrie, I think God has given me an idea that will help us. Long ago sailors used to sing songs to help them work. Maybe we could do the same."

"We could sing 'Row, Row, Row Your Boat,' "

Carrie said. So together they sang:
> "*Row*, row, *row* your boat
> *Gently* down the *stream*.
> *Merrily*, merrily, *merrily*, merrily,
> *Life* is but a *dream*."

They sang it slowly, rowing and dumping with the beat. Over and over they sang the song, looking at each other and grinning.

Pretty soon they turned into their cove. Carrie stopped singing to shout, "Look! There's our dock."

"Am I tired," Dad said, as he tied up the boat.

"But we weren't too tired to finish," Carrie said proudly. "And singing helped us work." ■

TIRED, BUT NOT TOO TIRED

From God's Word

Some sailed over the ocean
　　in ships.
They saw what the Lord can do,
　　his wonderful acts.
He commanded, and a
　　mighty wind began to blow
　　and stirred up the waves.
The ships were lifted high
　　in the air
　　and plunged down
　　into the depths.
In such danger the men
　　lost their courage;
then in their trouble they called
　　to the Lord,
　　and he saved them from
　　their distress . . .
　　and he brought them safe
　　to the port they wanted.
　　　—*from Psalm 107:23-30 (TEV)*

Think It Through

Ask your children these questions and discuss the answers.

1. Why was it important for Carrie to keep bailing the water out of the boat when she and her father were coming home?

2. How did God help them when they were in trouble? *He gave Carrie's dad an idea of how to make the work easier.*

3. How else could you turn hard work into a game? (Singing is one way.)

4. With your mom or dad, think of a job you have to do around the house that might be made easier if you could turn it into a game. What kind of a game or song might you use?

Books for you, containing stories to read aloud and discuss with your children

STORYBOOKS FOR *Caring* PARENTS

Scared, But Not Too Scared *(to think)*
Bored, But Not Too Bored *(to pretend)*
Angry, But Not Too Angry *(to talk)*
Tired, But Not Too Tired *(to finish)*